Teacher Mommy-Mommy Teacher

©Copyright 2020 by Jacqueline Jobes

Written work and activities were created by Jacqueline Jobes.

Teacher Mommy-Mommy Teacher LLC.

Photos Credit

Cover Page Image by Gerd Altmann from Pixabay

Rubik Cube, Duck, Submarine & Basketball Images by OpenClipart-Vectors from Pixabay

Bear, Cloudy, Rocking Horse & Boat Images by OpenClipart-Vectors from Pixabay

Fish Image by Michael Rühle from Pixabay

Truck, Blue and Red Ball, Train & Xylophone Images by Clker-Free-Vector-Images from Pixabay

Rain Cloud Image by Clker-Free-Vector-Images from Pixabay

Dinosaur Image by Mark Baird from Pixabay

Green and Purple Ball Images by Milu Černochová from Pixabay

Day & Night Images by M. Maggs from Pixabay

Green Meadow Image by MoteOo from Pixabay

Sun Image by DavidRockDesign from Pixabay

Snowy Day Image by bjt1958 from Pixabay

Heavy & Light Images by mohamed Hassan from Pixabay

Silhouette Image by johngelling from Pixabay

Elephant Image by Dmitry Abramov from Pixabay

Truck Image by Annalise Batista from Pixabay

Scale, Rock, and Car Image by Open Clipart-Vectors from Pixabay

Feather Image by gdakaska from Pixabay

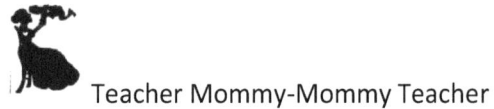
Teacher Mommy-Mommy Teacher

PRE-K MATH PROCESS CHARTS

Teacher Mommy-Mommy Teacher

Table of Content

Numbers 0-10 4-14

Shapes 15-25

Small, Medium & Large 26-28

Same & Different 29-30

Day & Night 31-32

Weather 33-36

Heavy & Light 37-38

Tall & Short 39

More or Less 40-41

Numbers, Number Names & Count 42-45

Number Chart 1-50 46

Hundred Chart 47

Part-Part-Whole (Number Bonds) 48

Month of the Year 49

Days of the Week 50

Telling Time 51

Calendar 52

Teacher Mommy-Mommy Teacher

zero

Teacher Mommy-Mommy Teacher

1 one

 Teacher Mommy-Mommy Teacher

 two

Teacher Mommy-Mommy Teacher

3 three

 four

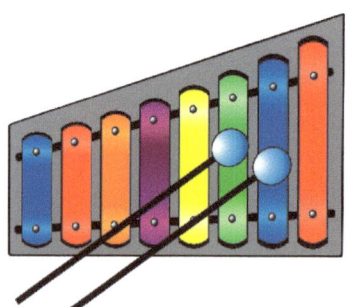

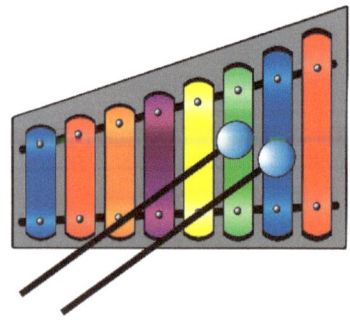 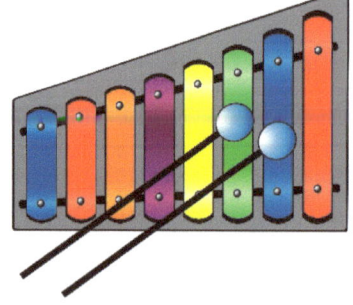 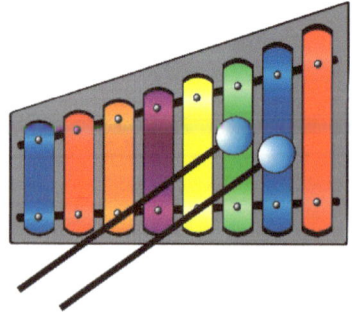

Teacher Mommy-Mommy Teacher

5 five

6 six

7 seven

Teacher Mommy-Mommy Teacher

eight

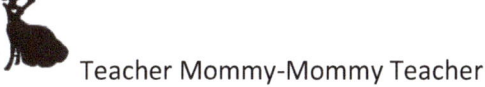

9 nine

Teacher Mommy-Mommy Teacher

10 ten

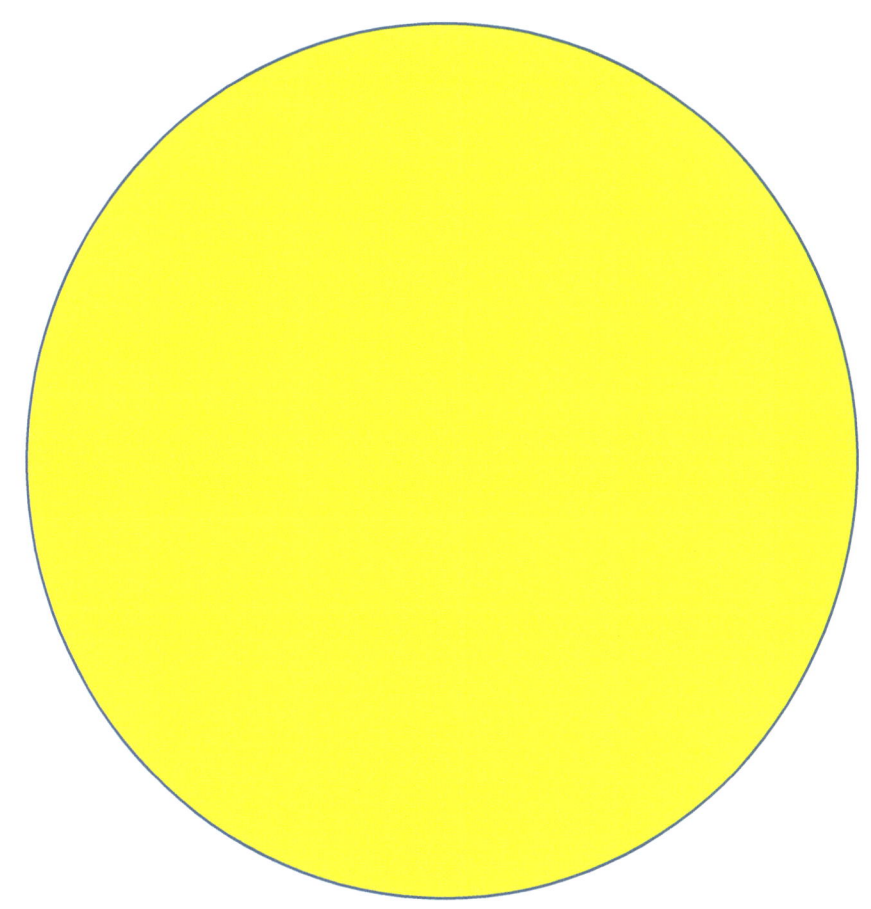

circle

Teacher Mommy-Mommy Teacher

square

triangle

diamond

rectangle

 Teacher Mommy-Mommy Teacher

oval

star

Teacher Mommy-Mommy Teacher

hexagon

 Teacher Mommy-Mommy Teacher

rhombus

 Teacher Mommy-Mommy Teacher

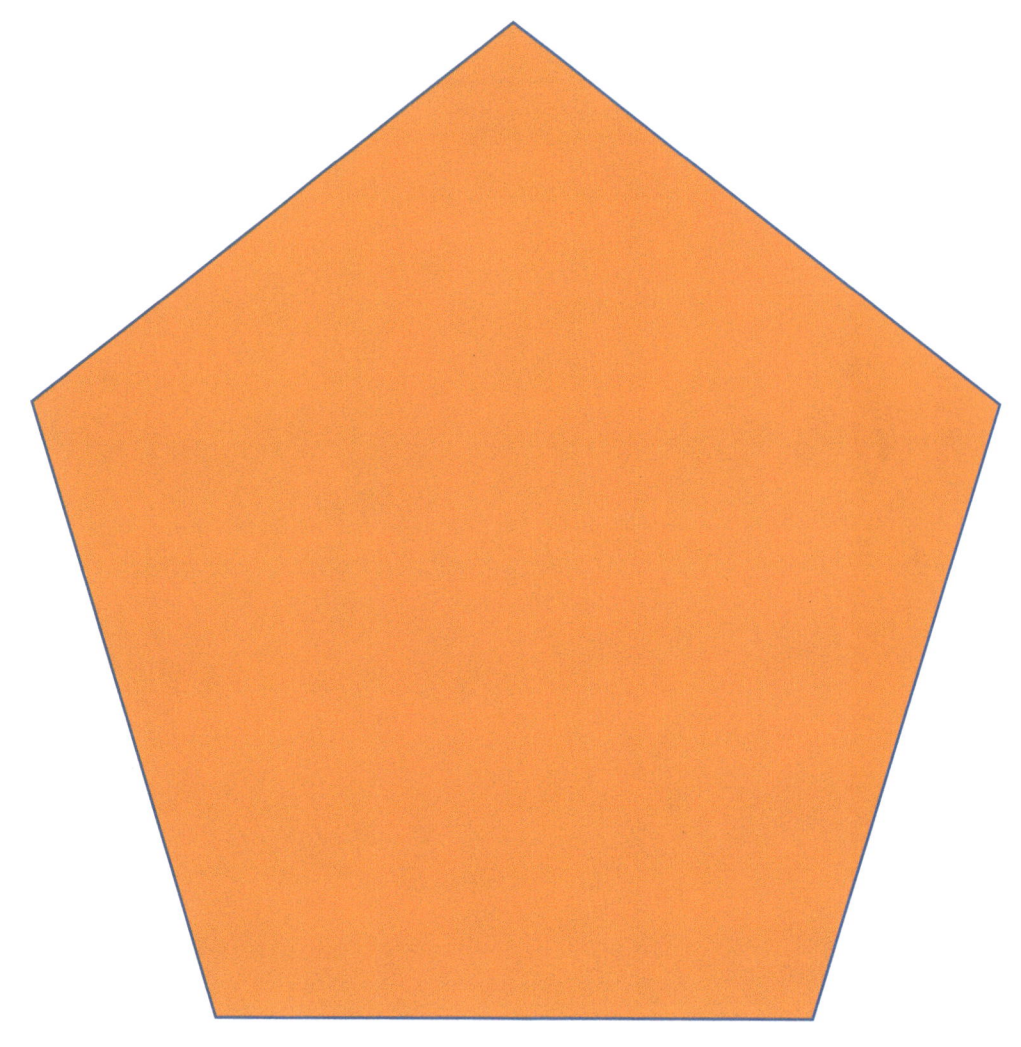

pentagon

Teacher Mommy-Mommy Teacher

octagon

small

medium

large

same

different

day

night

Teacher Mommy-Mommy Teacher

cloudy

sunny

Teacher Mommy-Mommy Teacher

rainy

snowy

heavy

Teacher Mommy-Mommy Teacher

light

Tall   Short

Teacher Mommy-Mommy Teacher

More or Less

More or Less

Numbers

Number	Number Names	Count
1	one	★
2	two	★★
3	three	★★★
4	four	★★★★
5	five	★★★★★
6	six	★★★★★★

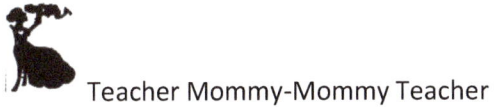

Numbers

Numbers	Number Names	Count
7	seven	💙💙💙💙 💙💙💙
8	eight	❤️❤️❤️❤️ ❤️❤️❤️❤️
9	nine	💚💚💚💚 💚 💚💚💚
10	ten	💜💜💜💜💜 💜💜💜💜💜
11	eleven	💛💛💛💛💛 💛💛💛💛💛💛
12	twelve	🤍🤍🤍🤍🤍 🤍🤍🤍🤍 🤍🤍🤍

Numbers

Number	Number Names	Count
13	thirteen	
14	fourteen	
15	fifteen	
16	sixteen	

Numbers

Number	Number Names	Count
17	seventeen	
18	eighteen	
19	nineteen	
20	twenty	

Numbers 1-50

1	2	3	4	5
6	7	8	9	10
11	12	13	14	15
16	17	18	19	20
21	22	23	24	25
26	27	28	29	30
31	32	33	34	35
36	37	38	39	40
41	42	43	44	45
46	47	48	48	50

Hundreds Chart

1	2	3	4	5	6	7	8	9	10
11	12	13	14	15	16	17	18	19	20
21	22	23	24	25	26	27	28	29	30
31	32	33	34	35	36	37	38	39	40
41	42	43	44	45	46	47	48	49	50
51	52	53	54	55	56	57	58	59	60
61	62	63	64	65	66	67	68	69	70
71	72	73	74	75	76	77	78	79	80
81	82	83	84	85	86	87	88	89	90
91	92	93	94	95	96	97	98	99	100

Part-Part-Whole (Number Bonds)

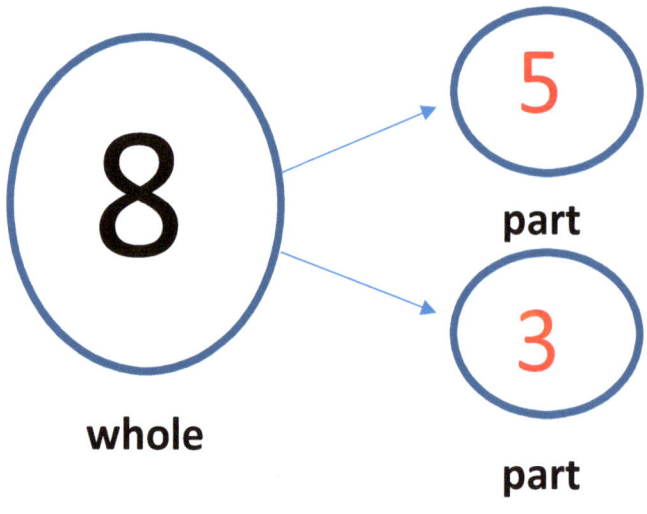

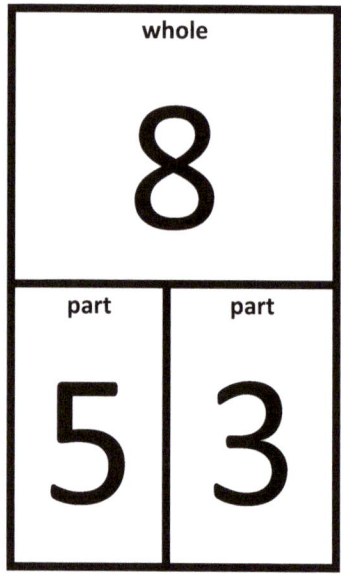

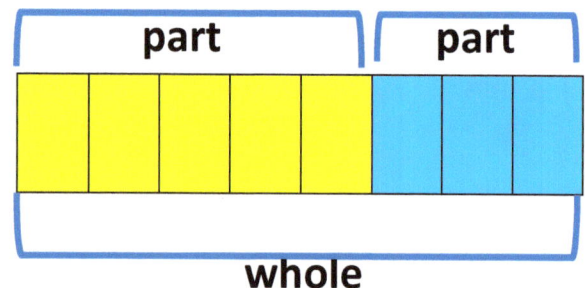

5+3=8

part + part = whole

8-5=3

whole − part = part

Months of the Year

- January
- February
- March
- April
- May
- June
- July
- August
- September
- October
- November
- December

Days of the Week

- Sunday
- Monday 
- Tuesday 
- Wednesday 
- Thursday 
- Friday 
- Saturday

Telling Time

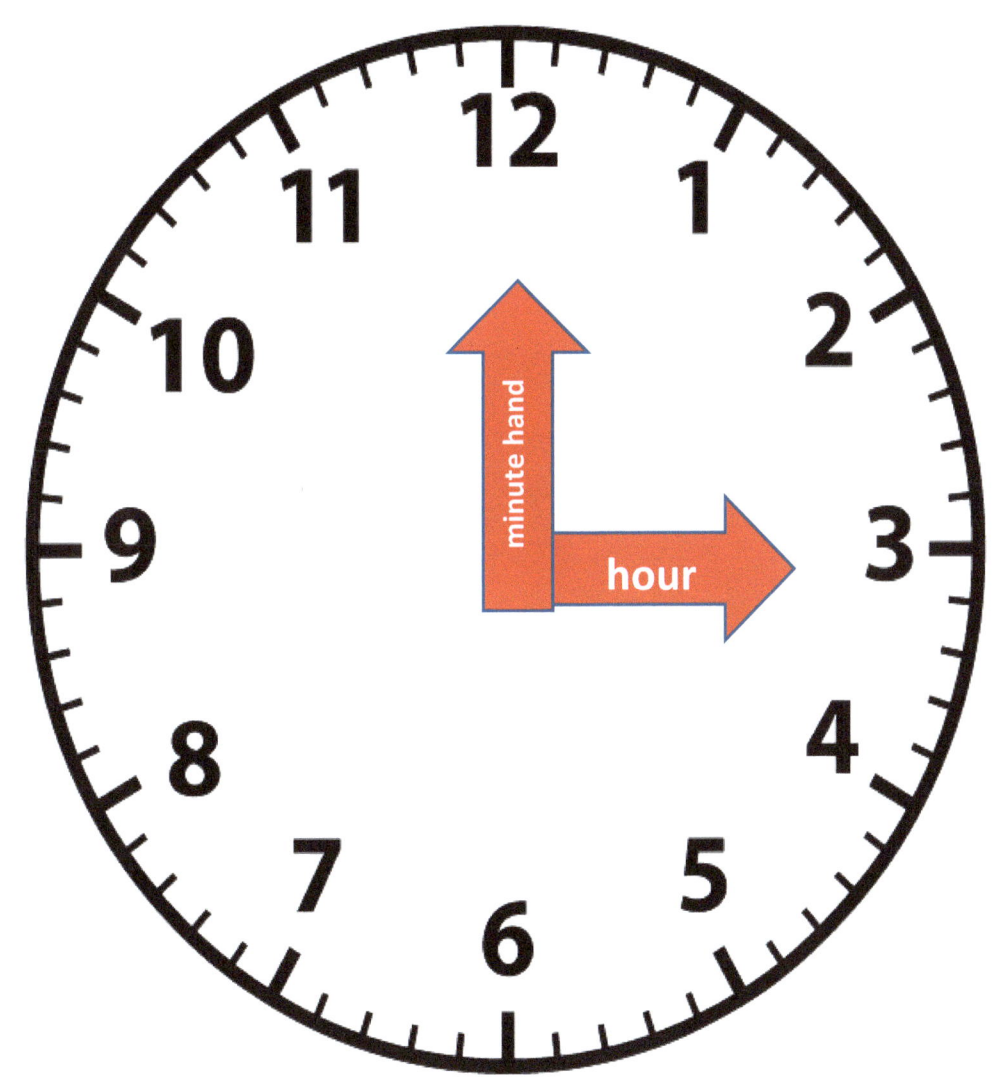

Teacher Mommy-Mommy Teacher

Calendar

August						
Sunday	Monday	Tuesday	Wednesday	Thursday	Friday	Saturday
						1
2	3	4	5	6	7	8
9	10	11	12	13	14	15
16	17	18	19	20	21	22
23	24	25	26	27	28	29
30	31					

www.ingramcontent.com/pod-product-compliance
Lightning Source LLC
Chambersburg PA
CBHW060758090426
42736CB00002B/68